USDA

United States
Department of
Agriculture

Forest Service

Pacific Northwest
Research Station

General Technical
Report
PNW-GTR-766

November 2008

# Factors Influencing Line Officers' Decisions About National Environmental Policy Act Project Design and Development

Donald G. MacGregor and David N. Seesholtz

## Authors

**Donald G. MacGregor** is a consultant, MacGregor-Bates, 1010 Villard Ave., Cottage Grove, OR 97424. **David N. Seesholtz** is a research liaison, U.S. Department of Agriculture, Forest Service, Pacific Northwest Research Station, Forestry Sciences Laboratory, 620 SW Main St., Suite 400, Portland, OR 97205.

## Cover Photo

Rolando Mendez, Deputy District Ranger on the Bend - Ft. Rock Ranger District, Deschutes National Forest

# Abstract

**MacGregor, Donald G.; Seesholtz, David N. 2008.** Factors influencing line
officers' decisions about National Environmental Policy Act project design and
development. Gen. Tech. Rep. PNW-GTR-766. Portland, OR: U.S. Department
of Agriculture, Forest Service, Pacific Northwest Research Station. 27 p.

Prior to the existence of the National Environmental Policy Act (NEPA), Forest
Service district rangers had considerable latitude to make resource management
decisions and execute management plans with relatively little encumbrance by documentation and process requirements. Today there appears to be differences not
only in the district ranger population, but in the decisionmaking processes they use
and how they adapt their management style to particular circumstances. Indepth
interviews were conducted with 12 district rangers to obtain their experiences with
project design and development, and how project planning is influenced by considerations about the NEPA process. District rangers appear to have changed their
management style to accommodate a shifting social and policy climate, and rangers
often view NEPA as a risk factor and as a process to be managed. Research methods
can be used to further analyze risk in terms of resource versus process risk, both of
which can potentially affect the agency in terms of opportunity and monetary costs,
efficiencies, and decision confidences.

Keywords: National Environmental Policy Act (NEPA), planning, land management decisionmaking, Forest Service.

# Introduction

Over the past four-plus decades, several studies have characterized the forest ranger position, starting with Kaufman's now-classic *The Forest Ranger* (1960). Using a set of five district rangers, Kaufman developed a profile of Forest Service rangers based on indepth interviews. His characterization of rangers as operating within a hierarchical structure to implement and execute agency policy objectives through decisionmaking at the local level portrays rangers as field executives primarily concerned with economy and efficiency. Thirty years later, Tipple and Wellman (1991) reviewed Kaufman's ranger profile and, based in part on Tipple's agency experience, noted that the emphasis on economy and efficiency had shifted toward representativeness (e.g., workforce issues) and responsiveness (e.g., public involvement vis-a-vis National Environmental Policy Act [NEPA] requirements). Subsequent studies using survey-type methodologies to characterize the line officer population, including district rangers, have identified shifts in ranger values over the period from approximately 1989 to 2004. Although line officers' perceptions of agency resource-use values changed sharply over that period, particularly for timber and water, line officers' personal judgments of resource-use values changed relatively little (Kennedy et al. 1992, 2005).

Research to date suggests that district rangers change their management style over time to accommodate a shifting social and policy climate, and that rangers are sensitive to the changing resource-use priorities within the agency. However, deeper questions about how district rangers adapt their unique management style to particular management circumstances have yet to be addressed. Although ranger perceptions appear sensitive to agency resource values, it is unclear how these perceptions along with other local management goals and objectives, as well as rangers' individual values, interact to determine the projects and activities that rangers choose (and choose not) to undertake.

The USDA Forest Service ranger districts are a focal point for the design and development of resource management projects to achieve the multiuse mission of the agency. Many of these projects involve the assessment and disclosure of environmental impacts under the requirements of NEPA. Since its inception in 1970, NEPA has called upon agency management and staff to undertake detailed analyses of their proposed management actions, the anticipated impacts of those actions, and (under some circumstances) the steps planned to mitigate unwanted or undesirable effects, and to submit their plans and analyses to public disclosure. The NEPA process is intended to help public officials make decisions that are based on understanding of environmental consequences, and take actions that protect, restore, and enhance the environment (NEPA 2003). Many projects succeed in the NEPA process; when they do, the investment in planning and analysis yields a return in terms of benefits to the natural resource base. Other projects succeed in NEPA but only after protracted appeals and litigation in which project opponents can stall or stop a proposed project through court or administrative actions. In these cases, the investment in planning and analysis may be relatively high, and unless the project return is commensurably high, the net value of the project may be dubious and the investment may offer little return. Finally, some projects fail in the NEPA process, in which case the investment is lost and the desired benefit to the resource base is foregone.

Although the original intent of NEPA was to ensure that projects planned by federal entities disclose environmental impacts of their actions and effects, legislation has resulted in planned projects being submitted to a potentially contentious process, the outcome of which may be uncertain at the time the project is conceptualized. At present, we have little understanding of how NEPA as an environmental disclosure process interacts with other processes inside ranger districts that relate to the design, development, and implementation of projects as part of units' natural resource management objectives. Is NEPA being used purely as an environmental disclosure process, or is it being used as a decisionmaking process for project design and development?

To address this question, an exploratory study was undertaken to better understand how resource management projects in ranger districts evolve from an initial idea or concept to project development and through the NEPA process. Twelve district rangers were interviewed concerning their experiences with project design and development, and how project planning is influenced by considerations about the NEPA process. Some of their direct quotes appear in the margins throughout this paper.

At present, there are 523 ranger districts in the National Forest System (Thompson 2007). A small handful of district rangers cannot be expected to provide a comprehensive and reliable picture of the relationship between project development and the NEPA process. The purpose of this study was to identify problem-framing concepts and hypotheses that provide useful guidance and direction for addressing the larger research question posed above.

**Many projects succeed in the NEPA process; when they do, the investment in planning and analysis yields a return in terms of benefits to the natural resource base.**

# Study Approach

## Ranger Identification and Selection

The rangers were selected from a database developed by identifying key informants who in the judgment of experienced district rangers and other line officers would provide useful information for the project. The initial database contained rangers from the nine geographic regions of the USDA Forest Service. Individuals were contacted by telephone and e-mail to solicit their support and involvement. The final selection of 12 individuals was based on several factors, including their geographic location, availability to be interviewed, and interest in the project. As much as possible, rangers were selected to provide regional diversity. Owing to time and availability constraints, it was difficult to include rangers from units in Southern and Eastern regions (e.g., Regions 8 and 9) and Alaska (Region 10). The final set of interviewees came from ranger districts in Western, Southwestern, Intermountain, Pacific Southwest, and Pacific Northwest (Regions 1, 3, 4, 5, and 6).

## Interview Process

Rangers were interviewed to elicit their backgrounds and experiences. Interviews were conducted at convenient locations, including unit offices, forest offices, or the interviewee's residence. Interviewees were given the opportunity to choose the location and to select a timeframe convenient to them. Interviews were scheduled to take approximately 1 to 1 1/2 hours.

An interview guide was prepared to provide a structure for the interviews and to lend continuity to the interview process. The guide was developed around four orienting themes:

- How projects are initially identified and selected.
- How a selected project concept is developed prior to any NEPA-related analyses.
- How projects are influenced by various aspects of NEPA.
- When during the process the management decision is made and the role of the environmental analysis.

Additional background information was collected as part of the interview process, including characteristics of the line officers and their career paths as well as characteristics and management complexities of their units. The actual conduct of the interview was varied to take advantage of interviewee responses and to allow for opportunities to adapt the interviews contingent on what was learned as the interviews progressed. Interview content was analyzed to identify themes, concepts, and information of value for framing further study.

## Findings

**District rangers and the management context: sources of variance—**
Significant differences may exist in terms of district rangers and the context of the units they manage. Although degrees in forestry, natural resource management, and other natural sciences have been the traditional education preparation for rangers, there is more diversity in educational background and experience in the ranger population today (Koontz 2007). Rangers and other agency personnel are being asked to play a much different role than in the past as social values are at the heart of many of the environmental issues they manage. However, most managers are traditionally unprepared to deal with such value-laden issues and the consensus-building process needed in decisionmaking to successfully implement land management decisions (Magill 1991, Martin et al. 1996). Public administration, business administration, social science, and other non-natural science degrees provide the advanced educational preparation for some rangers. The type of educational preparation a manager receives may influence how they approach their role as a line officer and the relative emphasis they give to various aspects of the position. For example, those with forestry degrees will be oriented to appreciate the natural resource aspects of the position. Those with educational background in, for example, social or administrative sciences may approach the position from a fundamental appreciation of the social aspects of resource management. An education in business administration may uniquely attune the line officer to the business management aspects of the position.

How rangers enter into the line officer career path can differ considerably. Some rangers are identified by their managers as having the characteristics and qualities that would make them a good ranger candidate and are mentored for the position. This tends to follow the traditional pathway in the agency, by which line officers were identified by senior line officers and specifically mentored into the line officer community. Although formal mentoring programs are virtually gone from the agency today, this tradition still exists and is a means by which many line officers achieve their initial entry.

Others desiring a ranger career take steps on their own toward achieving that position. These steps may involve openly expressing to the line officer their interest in becoming a ranger. They may seek temporary line officer positions or deputy positions that place them in a line officer role where they can obtain knowledge and experience.

It is not uncommon for some rangers to be either unsure of their ranger qualifications or have no specific line officer career plans, yet become rangers after occupying the position on a temporary assignment. Changes over the past two decades in how the agency identifies and develops its line officers have tended to create multiple pathways by which individuals reach the line officer position.

*"I put a lot of value on people taking their time to get to this position."*

The experience base of rangers differs and is changing from the traditional background in timber management and related activities. Some rangers have a strong NEPA background, perhaps the result of one or more staff positions as, for example, a planner or interdisciplinary (ID) team leader. Others do not and rely heavily on unit staff members, for example, to provide detailed knowledge and experience in the NEPA process. Rangers differ in how they perceive the district ranger position in the context of their overall agency career objectives. Some rangers view the position as a step on the line officer career ladder and regard their district ranger role as entry level. These individuals may actively seek promotion to, for example, forest-level positions and remain in one location for a relatively short period. Other rangers view the position as a desirable career end point and choose to remain in their current position and location, or relatively close by. This latter group may make significant progress in developing strong community relations as a result of their long tenure in their location. This group may also have strong ties to direct involvement in resource management decisionmaking, and place a high value on observing the results of their management efforts in terms of direct action on the ground and the ultimate outcomes and changes to the natural resources they are managing. Their tenure may also afford them the ability to develop a strong working relationship with staff and take greater advantage of staff expertise and training in the skills relating to the NEPA process. Along these same lines, rangers who occupy their position for longer periods may achieve a higher level of team integration among staff members and communicate more efficiently about the management direction (and projects) they seek to pursue, as well as forge projects that move more quickly from concept to analysis and documentation.

*"Our society is so incredibly polarized that no matter what decision we make there are going to be those that love you and those that hate you and then there are those in the middle, and you have to be okay with that."*

The perceived qualities of what constitutes a good ranger (or ranger candidate) differ. The ability to communicate well with both agency and stakeholders ranks high with some. For others, liking to work with people is a primary qualification. A strong capability, willingness, and desire to develop collaborative relationships with the public and other nongovernmental stakeholders is perceived to be a hallmark of good ranger qualifications. Technical knowledge or skill in dealing with the NEPA process is seldom, if ever, seen as a quality required to be a good ranger.

The management style of district rangers differs in many ways. With regard to staff, some rangers may have a very hands-off style in which they encourage staff (i.e., disciplinary specialists) to freely generate and identify projects for the unit. Open solicitation for project ideas may even extend to clerical staff and others on the unit not directly involved in a resource area. This style of management emphasizes inclusiveness and involvement of unit personnel. Rangers having this management style may also place higher importance on a consensus style of project development, whereby agreement among staff and line is a significant barometer for when a project has achieved the right scope and level of detail in its environmental analysis.

*"It's critical that rangers be able to visualize solutions for issues and problems and methods of operation."*

Other rangers may prefer a hands-on style of management in which project development is undertaken in the context of a more rigorous planning process that is strongly led by the ranger. This category of rangers may have more experience with planning processes as, for example, part of their pre-ranger assignments as a staff specialist. How the ranger interacts with and manages staff may be related to the strength and qualifications of their ID team leader as well as the number and qualifications of staff on their unit. For some rangers, the level of NEPA background and expertise on their unit may be of significant concern.

Resource management contexts may differ considerably in terms of unit characteristics (e.g., staffing, budget), resource management complexity, and sociopolitical factors. Although commonalities between units exist, each unit has its own set of management challenges, some owing to the resource base and some owing to the social context within which the unit must operate. Project selection and development, to be successful, takes account of both the variable needs of the resource base as well as the social environment within which the project is to be implemented.

*"The biggest (source of) complexity we have is staffing; it's funding, which relates to having adequate numbers of resource staff to carry on the job."*

The process by which a particular ranger is chosen to manage a particular agency unit is not explicit and well defined. Rangers may tend to self-select themselves into management situations according to their own values and career goals, the opportunities that present themselves, and the needs of the upper level managers (e.g., forest supervisors) who select them. The idiosyncratic nature of this process suggests that the concept of "fit" between a ranger and their resource management context may be a useful way to understand how and why the NEPA process may be, for example, more efficient in some districts than others.

Assessing ranger districts and the potential fit with the characteristics of their managers requires criteria or standards by which this can be gauged. Efficiency is, potentially, one such standard. Although the efficiency of the NEPA process is generally discussed as important to improving how the agency deals with NEPA, systems and measures for addressing efficiency require refinement and specification (Jesse 1998, Luther 2005, USDA Forest Service 2002). Several potential measures of efficiency present themselves, based on the general notion that time and cost considerations are important to make the best use of unit resources. For example, cost to achieve the completion of a NEPA analysis might be one indicator of efficiency. Another might be the time required to move from an initial project concept to a completed environmental assessment (EA). Communication between line management and staff, as well as communication between staff members constitute the basis for another set of potential measures. We conjecture that the development of suitable measures and methods for assessing NEPA efficiency will be most productive if focused on multidimensional indicators that take into consideration time, cost, and stylistic aspects of management. These indicators should account for not only the economic efficiency associated with a particular NEPA project, but also the efficiency achieved by the planning aspects of unit management that include the scoping and staging of multiple projects developed over time. Additionally, more attention needs to be placed on evaluating the substantive purpose and outcome of the process in evaluating or measuring efficiency (Cashmore 2004).

**Source and scope of project concepts—**
Project concepts may be generated in a number of ways and come from a number of sources. The Land Management Plan (LMP) process provides an overarching context for project concepts, and candidate concepts must, by policy, fit within this framework. How project concepts are identified and developed may differ with ranger district and with individual rangers' management style (Yaffee 1999). In general, project concepts can be subjected to a number of influence factors that push them to becoming either larger or smaller in scope and complexity. The following tabulation lists some of the factors that influence project scope:

**The development of suitable measures and methods for assessing NEPA efficiency will be most productive if focused on multidimensional indicators that take into consideration time, cost, and stylistic aspects of management.**

| Promote larger projects | Promote smaller projects |
| --- | --- |
| Multiuse agency mission | NEPA process considerations |
| Interdisciplinary perspective | Unidimensional project objectives |
| Economic efficiency | Issue-focused environmental opposition |
| Systemic view of the ecology | Disciplinary isolation of staff |
| Perceived need to involve staff members | Limitations on funding resources |
| Line officer incentive and promotion system | Healthy Forest Restoration Act (HFRA) and Health Forest Initiative (HFI) |
| Planning approaches | Targets |
| General public support for the agency and its mission | Hot-button issues |

"Targets" (both soft and hard) are one possible common source of projects. Target-based projects may come from an upper level management unit (e.g., forest, region) and may or may not be directly linked to the LMP. Project concepts may come from outside the agency in the form of permits or requests to use or impact the resource base; examples include requests for mining permits, grazing permits, and the routing of electrical power or natural gas transmission lines.

Staff can also be an important source of project concepts, with identification based on disciplinary considerations or observations of, for example, the presence of risks to the resource base or the need to improve forest health. Staff-generated initial project concepts may or may not be integrated across disciplinary specialties when presented to the line officer for consideration, depending on several factors including (a) how well the various disciplines working on a unit are able to communicate and develop integrated project concepts independent of line officer involvement, and (b) the experience and capabilities of the local ID team leader. More or less work and effort may need to be undertaken by the district ranger to shape staff-generated projects and to integrate them across disciplinary lines if needed.

Projects may be initiated and developed by district rangers to improve or enhance community relations. Although some of these projects may have only an indirect relationship to the natural resource base, they are possibly perceived to improve the relationship between public stakeholders and the agency, with the anticipated result that natural resource projects will encounter a more receptive sociopolitical environment during the NEPA process. Projects along these lines and that provide what the district ranger sees as the necessary social base for

*"(I'm looking for) somebody that isn't narrow minded or thinking: I'm going to plow the deep roads for wildlife. I'm going to fight the good fight for my species."*

resource projects may take significant time and effort that factor into the calendar time required to develop and implement NEPA projects.

Rangers may inherit partially completed projects from their predecessors. These projects may have partially completed environmental analyses associated with them, and a significant investment may have already been made in moving the project through various parts of the NEPA process. The rationale for the project may not be clear and staff may not fully understand what the previous line officer intended by pursuing a particular project and its alternatives. Reconstructing the project and its logic can be time consuming. Abandoning the project altogether can be problematic from a staff management perspective, particularly if significant effort has already been invested.

**The NEPA process: two faces of NEPA—**
The NEPA may be viewed as both (a) a process to be managed and (b) as a risk factor in the management of other unit processes. With regard to NEPA as a process to manage, rangers may tend to refer to the "NEPA Triangle" as a normative or prescriptive basis for structuring and guiding the work required to move a project through its NEPA elements (fig. 1). However, the linear approach to project development suggested by the NEPA process may not describe well the actual process by which project concepts evolve and are carried through to a decision and implementation.

Rangers may engage in an iterative process by which a project concept is narrowed and sharpened through several cycles (fig. 2). Some of these cycles may include the development, review, and refinement of, for example, an environmental analysis to improve project factors such as clarity, feasibility, and information content. Reducing sources of uncertainty may be a key aspect of the iterative process. Ranger management of the process and interactions with staff during the process may serve as a basis for ranger confidence in the overall decision process. Communication between the ranger and the various staff specialists involved in a project may make up a significant portion of the effort associated with developing a project and carrying it through the NEPA process.

The process of project iteration may be reflected in changes to the scope and complexity of project, with the project sometimes growing larger and then smaller in response to the influence factors discussed above. As the project begins to center on the appropriate scope and complexity, a consensus is approached by line and staff that the project is "right." From a management perspective, it is perceived desirable that a window of time is allowed for this to take place, and projects

*"When a specialist is a part of a team and they know that their ideas are valuable, the risk of being careless goes down substantially."*

*"The uncertainty that causes me to pause before I make a decision . . . is the background that shows how (the staff) got to the findings."*

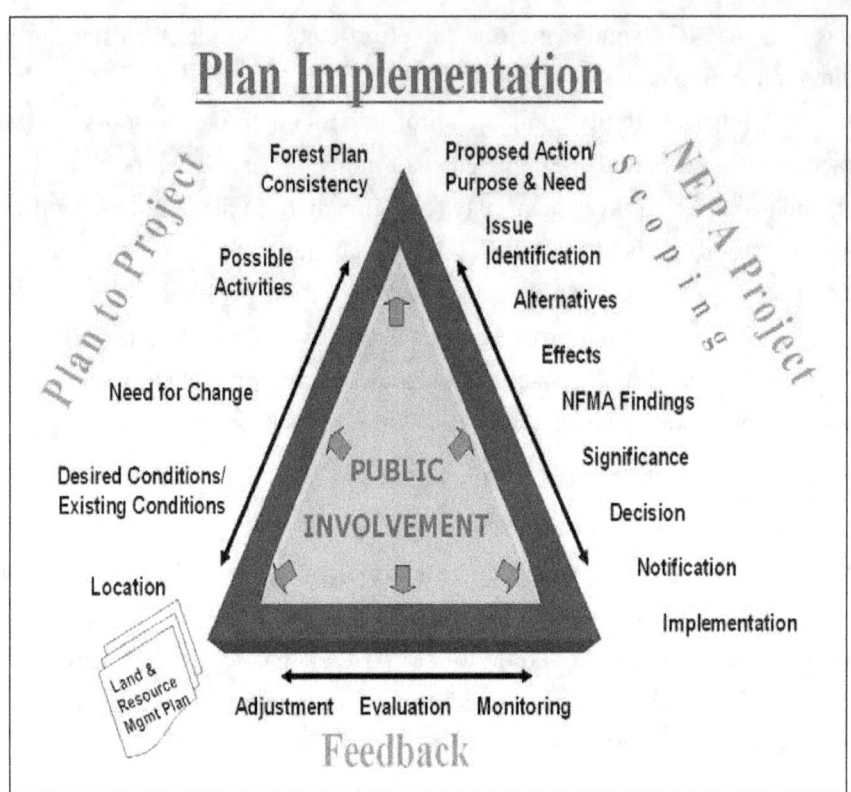

Figure 1—The NEPA Triangle. (Source: USDA Forest Service 2007).

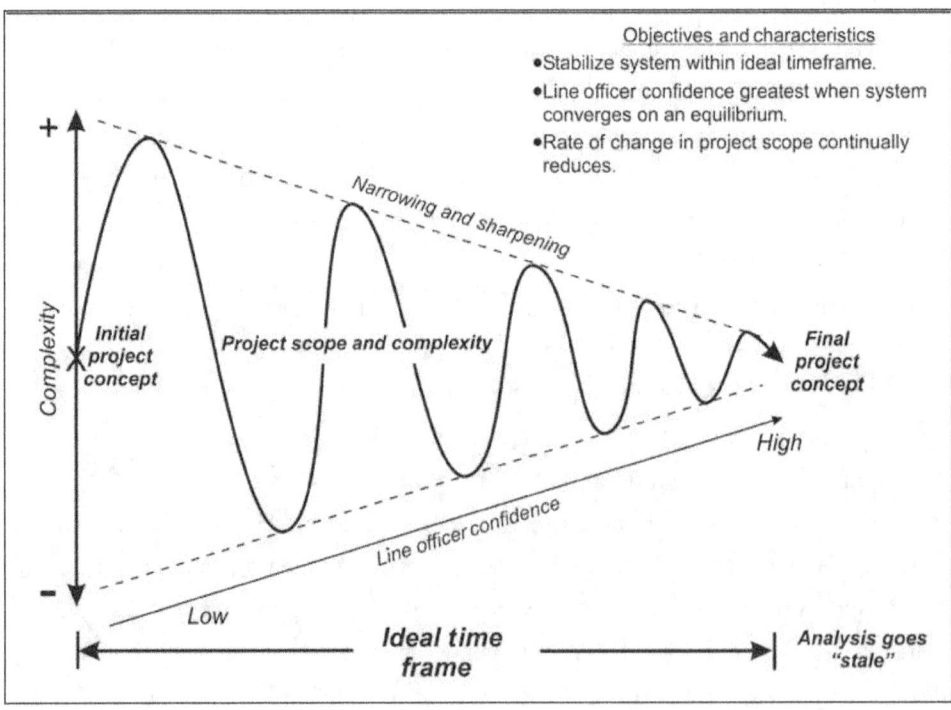

Figure 2—Iterative model of project development.

should not be developed too quickly nor take too long. Projects that settle on an equilibrium too quickly are perceived to be at risk owing to insufficient planning and thought. Projects that take too long may have entered into, for example, areas of analysis where staff cannot agree upon the nature or scope of impacts.

The NEPA is often viewed as a risk factor in the management of other unit processes. The uncertain outcome of the NEPA process (e.g., no appeal, appeal, litigation) may result in a significant time lag between when a project is conceptualized and when it is finally implemented. In some cases, the project may not move forward at all. These outcomes can result in both economic and noneconomic impacts to the unit. These are discussed in more detail below.

### The "NEPA sieve" and project selection—

National Environmental Policy Act considerations influence project selection at the earliest stages, and tend to be used as a first-cut NEPA sieve to determine which projects to move forward in the NEPA process. Line officers may differ in how they structure and apply the NEPA sieve. Public land managers have considerable flexibility in how a project proposal is designed and may use this discretion to design a project that has greater social acceptability (Laband et al. 2006). Projects may be divided into two, three, or perhaps four categories as part of an initial screening and selection process, with one category for projects that are deemed unlikely to make it through the NEPA process.

The remaining categories may define projects that require, to varying degrees, line officer involvement as part of the overall development approach. In these cases, line officer involvement may include significant efforts to garner additional sociopolitical resources, or efforts to involve higher level unit management (e.g., forest supervisor) to obtain, for example, broader ownership for the project.

Rangers will at times and under varying conditions undertake relatively high-risk NEPA projects. Management strategies for these projects include (a) careful attention to project definition and scope, (b) additional communication with staff members to clarify its high-risk nature and to improve staff ownership for the range of potential NEPA-related outcomes, and (c) additional interaction and communication with agency and nonagency stakeholders.

### Definitions of risk in project selection and development—

Risk is a central consideration in the management of many activities and enterprises. From a technical standpoint, risk is generally conceptualized in terms of two components: a potential consequence or loss, and the probability or likelihood that the potential loss will occur. The result is a definition of risk based on the principle

*"I'm pretty sure this is the right way to go, but would another person looking at the same (environmental analysis) but without the knowledge I have, come to the same conclusion?"*

*"I think that as line officers what we're really called upon to do is manage risk."*

*"A lot of it comes down to what is it that's going to move the resource in the direction it ought to be moved; the best weighing of process risk against resource risk."*

**For natural resource managers, one form of risk assessment pertains to risks to the natural resource base, which we will refer to here as resource risk.**

of expected value, by which the loss is multiplied by its associated probability of occurrence to provide a measure of risk (Kaplan and Garrick 1981). By this measure, risk is the probability-weighted value attached to a negative outcome or loss, the determination of which involves two dimensions: one associated with the consequence itself, and the other associated with its likelihood.

Because virtually all human activities involving decisionmaking have uncertain outcomes, and outcomes have the potential to result in loss, risk is an important consideration in decisionmaking independent of whether it can be formalized in terms of the expected value calculus noted above. Indeed, from a large body of research spanning a great number of decisionmaking domains, it appears that although people consider risk in their decisions, there is little evidence that they do so according to a technical standard of risk (Montgomery et al. 2004). Line officers are no exception in this regard, even though the concept of risk is one they consider and is a term that they use regularly to describe how they evaluate project decisions.

In real-world decision problems, matters of risk often become complex. Technical approaches can be applied to complex problems to yield structured and quantitative models of risk (Haimes 1998). However, these can be costly and time consuming to develop even when all of the factors are known. From an informal standpoint, risk can be considered in terms of a multidimensional framework by which different risk factors are evaluated as part of decisionmaking. For natural resource managers, one form of risk assessment pertains to risks to the natural resource base, which we will refer to here as **resource risk.** Resource risk is any potential loss to the natural resource base. In essence, resource management has as one of its principal goals the management of resource risk through its various monitoring and intervention processes. Potential losses to the resource base can result from natural disturbance factors such as fire, disease, and noxious vegetation. It can also result from human activities such as arson or chemical releases from mining operations. Active management to control such factors and their effects on the resource base constitutes risk management, a process that involves the identification of risk sources, an assessment of their impacts on the resource base, the determination of a desired adjustment to the risk, and the development and implementation of an appropriate management response.[1] One form that management response to resource risk can take is projects developed and implemented with the objective

---

[1] For a more detailed discussion of risk management as applied to ecosystem management, see Cleaves and Haynes (1999).

of taking action on the land to reduce resource risk or manage the level of risk. Such projects are almost always subjected to the NEPA process before they can be conducted.

The NEPA process itself poses uncertainties to the management of resource risk, as the ultimate approval of a NEPA project is influenced by judicial and administrative factors that are out of the direct control of the line officer and unit staff. Should a project fail for either judicial or administrative reasons, the potential benefits in terms of resource risk management (e.g., risk reduction) are lost.

The overall evaluation of projects with respect to the challenges posed by NEPA involves an assessment of **process risk**. Process risk is the potential for a project to fail owing to one or more of the process elements associated with NEPA. In practice, this is often conceptualized to be the litigation and appeal aspects of NEPA whereby the courts and other administrative bodies are afforded the opportunity to oppose a project. Process risk can also be associated with the analytic requirements for a NEPA project and the inability of the unit to adequately identify and scope an environmental analysis such that the project rationale is coherent. A portion of projects requiring a NEPA analysis (i.e., EA or Environmental Impact Statement [EIS]) are entered into but not completed on account of various problems associated with staffing levels, loss of project continuity during analysis, changing environmental conditions, changing sociopolitical conditions, and changes in unit management.

Process risk is an informal assessment. At present, the agency has no formalized basis for assessing process risk and does not have a common definition among district rangers. Terms such as litigation risk and implementation risk are also used to convey the notion that the NEPA process, both directly and indirectly, exposes the unit to the potential for loss. How process risk is assessed may differ from one ranger to another, and from one time to another for a given ranger depending on several factors, including (a) the particular type of project being considered (e.g., fire salvage, recreation, stream restoration), (b) staff capabilities and experience, (c) the past and present sociopolitical climate, (d) past and recent court rulings, and (e) the management context within which the ranger is currently working (e.g., forest, region, agency). Because of this, the assessment of process risk is subjected to many sources of variability, all of which contribute to a lack of consistency in how NEPA projects are developed.

Process risk is considered early in the project selection and as well during the entire project development. At different times in project development the assessment of process risk can take on alternative characterizations. For example, a

*"You've got to weigh your resource risks very carefully; you want to make the right decisions on the resource. That's our primary job. The process risk you take is to go through the process in such a way that you get to do the right thing on the ground as a professional."*

**Process risk is considered early in the project selection and as well during the entire project development.**

*"(The) project that's in litigation and negotiation now is 11 years old. My fear with the settlement is that the ground has changed and we're negotiating it on an 11-year-old NEPA document that doesn't represent what's out there anymore. Over that length of time I lost the original players. I'm the only original player."*

*"If it's an analysis you have to go back into, it's a whole lot of time and effort that could have been spent creating something that was going to actually happen on the ground."*

project idea or concept may be evaluated initially in terms of its essential survivability through the NEPA process, with high-risk projects being rejected. At other times in the project development cycle, process risk vis-a-vis NEPA, may be pitted against other risks that are associated with unit management. For example, disciplinary compartmentalization could make it difficult to develop cross-disciplinary communication in project development. Staging projects to reduce complexity exposes the line officer to the risk that some staff specialists may perceive themselves as left out of the project development cycle, or that their particular specialty is underappreciated in terms of its role in resource management. Attempting to be excessively inclusive of staff specialties in the development of a project could increase its complexity (and its NEPA process risk) but may decrease the risk of staff alienation. Significant management resources in terms of ranger and staff time may be applied to the management (and minimization) of process risk. This is discussed in more detail in a later section.

**Process risk and potential losses to the unit—**
Process risk arises because the NEPA process directly and indirectly exposes a unit, its staff, and its management to the potential for significant losses, both economic and noneconomic. These losses can take various forms.

One form of loss is that associated with **opportunity costs**. Opportunity costs (or losses) occur when one project is chosen for development over another, but the chosen project fails to be implemented owing to NEPA-related factors. The anticipated value of the foregone project represents an **opportunity loss** in that the benefit of the project is not realized. In addition, if the upfront development costs or investment for the chosen project is greater than the unchosen project, then that difference is lost as well. Opportunity costs are not formally evaluated in the agency. Although some rangers consider opportunity costs in selecting projects for development and for carrying through the NEPA process, there appears to be no formalized assessment of these costs in considering the overall value of pursuing one project over another.

Loss or delay of funding owing to the NEPA process may be a significant loss to a unit. Many projects carry with them a revenue stream when the project is implemented. These revenues may be required to support, for example, staff operations as well as general facility expenses. The loss of revenue owing to a failure of the project in the NEPA process can have financial impacts on a unit. For example, maintaining consistency in staff full-time equivalents is an important management consideration for district rangers. Variation in unit funding can affect a unit's staff budget, with resulting changes in the unit's staffing profile.

Maintaining unit and staff morale is critical to maintaining the capabilities needed to succeed in resource management. Modern resource management is a team endeavor and requires the cooperative efforts of a cadre of disciplinary specialists as well as guiding management to fulfill the multiuse mission of the agency. Achieving a high level of team cooperation and efficiency necessitates a concomitantly high morale. The failure of projects in the NEPA process can lead to low morale. A sense of loss may occur if, for example, a canceled project is perceived as an indicator of the unit's capabilities. It may also occur if the unit has a high level of investment in implementing the project and a strong desire to see action taken on the ground. Line officers may be particularly sensitive to this issue and may avoid projects that could lead to disappointment. Although the loss of a single project to NEPA-related factors may have relatively little impact on unit morale, repeated or successive project failures can be problematic from a staff management perspective.

The line officer's perception of his or her image as an effective leader and manager may play a significant role in the decisions they make with respect to project development and the NEPA process. With respect to staff, line officers may actively seek to maintain a positive image as a good leader who makes sound decisions about project selection. With respect to nonagency stakeholders and the general public, line officers may desire to be seen as exemplifying high-quality leadership with regard to resource management decisionmaking. Losses owing to elements of the NEPA process, and particularly appeals and litigation, may be seen as compromising their image as an effective leader and manager. This is an aspect of the line officer role that may be underappreciated in the realm of NEPA as a disclosure process. In general, many of the "soft" elements of unit management may be underappreciated and need to be discussed more fully.

**Approaches and strategies for management of process risk—**
How risk management is approached will depend on a number of factors, including the level of risk that is acceptable to a manager. Acceptability is a varying concept and will depend on the risk attitudes of an individual, as well as the ways in which risk-based decision problems are analyzed and framed (Fischhoff et al. 1981). Risk management can be seen as an adaptive management response to situations in which there is a potential for loss. In general, people seek to maintain equilibrium with respect to risk and will exercise management actions that are consistent with adjusting their present risk conditions to a level that represents a desirable or target level of risk (Wilde 2001).

*"Staff morale is a huge factor. I leave (a project) open for everybody to hook on and have some owner- ship. . . The range of alternatives is how I think everybody is able to hook on (to the project) and own it."*

*"You lose a lot of face if you fail with your analysis."*

*"My strategy is to manage a process so that the controversy is simply a difference of opinion on what the right answer is; it's not based on analysis differences. I don't feel a lot of uncertainty when I've been active in that process."*

Risk management is a cyclical process that involves (a) assessment of risk, (b) comparing perceived to desired level of risk, (c) determining the required risk adjustment, (d) selecting a risk management strategy, (e) implementing the strategy, and finally (f) monitoring and evaluating the result (fig. 3). Active management of process risk involves all of these steps in one form or another, though they may not be open and explicit, and may take on a different form in different situations and by different line officers.

A general strategy can be described in terms of a dynamic risk assessment and management model in which managerial experience and style forms the basis for a desired level of process risk. This level of process risk is compared with a perceived level of process risk to yield a risk adjustment. One or more strategies for process risk management are selected and applied, with the outcome monitored in terms of its impact on perceived process risk. The feedback loop in the model operates to bring about and maintain a concordance between the desired level of process risk and the level of process risk that is perceived to exist. The effectiveness of the model is contingent upon a number of managerial factors, including the personal risk attitudes of the manager (e.g., risk taking, loss aversion), the decisionmaking skills and style of the manager, and ability to implement the management strategy.

In general, active management of process risk can be accomplished by several means, including:

- **Rejection of high process risk projects**: Line officers may reject projects for consideration that are perceived to have excessively high process risk. The strategy by which this assessment is made may not be consistent across rangers. Projects that are rejected may include activities such as fire salvage, road construction, projects in roadless areas, projects in threatened and endangered species areas, and old-growth logging. However, there appear to be no universally defined criteria for high-risk projects, and one ranger may undertake a project that another ranger would not. The judgment that a project is too high-risk to undertake may have important perceptual qualities that differ depending on such factors as the capability of staff, current conditions with respect to stakeholder concerns, and the relative benefits of implementing the project.
- **Decreased project scope and complexity**: More complex projects, such as those attempting to accomplish multiple resource objectives under a single project umbrella, may be seen by some rangers as exposing them to greater

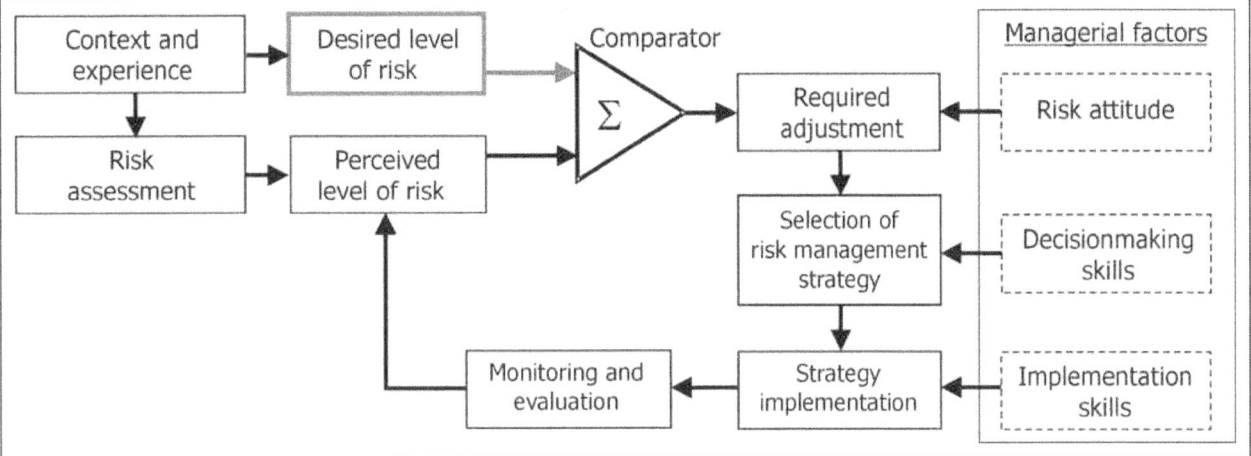

Figure 3—Dynamic model of process risk assessment and risk management.

risk by allowing more opportunities for project opponents to identify technical and procedural weaknesses or flaws. Rangers may avoid programmatic or landscape-scale projects if they perceive that such projects introduce complexities (e.g., cumulative impacts) that could lead to delay or rejection of the project as part of the NEPA process. This strategy may come into conflict with other agency principles or concepts such as programmatic project development, landscape-scale project development, and ecosystem-scale project development.

- **Increase the depth and rigor of environmental analyses***:* An important and often-used strategy for process risk management is to increase the level of effort applied to NEPA-related documentation, particularly environmental analyses. This may occur as part of an initial environmental assessment in response to perceived process risk, or in response to a successful appeal by project opponents. From the standpoint of process efficiency, a key concern here is the potential for a "sunk-cost effect" to occur with respect to a NEPA project and its associated analysis. A sunk-cost effect occurs when additional resources are expended on a project beyond what would have been spent if that amount had been known beforehand (Arkes and Blumer 1985, Arkes and Hutzel 2000). The result is a continuous increase in resource expenditures (e.g., staff time) on, for example, deepening and refining an EA to a level that would not have been considered reasonable and justifiable were that amount of depth proposed at the beginning of the project. Sunk-cost effects occur because of a judgmental bias arising from how people evaluate prospects that involve a sure loss (i.e., the sunk cost already expended) against the possibility of avoiding that loss by expending additional resources (Kahneman and Tversky 1979). The sunk-cost effect tends to amplify the perception of risk associated with the project, and the need to take action to reduce and manage that risk. Managing the appropriate level of depth in an analysis can be of key concern to a line officer, and staff may be of the opinion that more analysis is appropriate than the line officer believes is required. Management of process risk carries with it additional risks that express themselves in terms of line and staff relations.

- **Portfolio development:** Rangers may seek to manage process risk by developing portfolios of projects that provide a form of diversification with respect to, for example, process risk. The concept of risk diversification is a central feature of modern portfolio theory, and in efficient portfolios, overall portfolio risk is reduced by managing for uncorrelated risk in the portfolio mix. **Uncorrelated risk** means that should one project or prospect fail, that failure is not linked or correlated to the potential for failure of other projects in the portfolio. In essence, all of one's eggs are not in one basket. For portfolio development to meet its desired ends, the portfolio developer must be careful to assess the respective risks of each of their projects or investments and determine to what degree the risk is from a common source (systematic risk), and to what degree the risk for each project is unrelated to that for other projects (specific risk).[2] It is unclear how this strategy is operationalized by district rangers and whether their intuitively constructed portfolios are indeed reducing overall portfolio risk, or whether their portfolio collections of projects are correlated with respect to risk, in which case overall risk may be increased.

- **Decomposed and staged plans of work that involve sequential projects:** Breaking down relatively large resource management plans into smaller, less complex projects is one approach rangers may take to reduce process risk. However, some rangers may have experienced difficulties with this approach if a significant number of small projects interact to produce cumulative impacts that are only observable by examining the entire set

*"Specialists don't always feel that line is taking into consideration their input. So, my role as a line officer is to develop the skills to make all the input valuable."*

---

[2] For the historical derivation of portfolio theory, see Markowitz (1959). For an accessible discussion of portfolio theory in the context of modern economics, see Bernstein (1998).

of projects. Likewise, the staging and timing of small projects may be difficult to rationalize, thereby increasing the process risk associated with the overall set of projects. Planning approaches used by ranger districts may or may not give adequate consideration to the interactive and cumulative effects of small projects. This strategy for managing process risk can be seen as a form of portfolio development where a given project is segmented into a series of smaller projects. Here, the problem of correlated risks may be important to evaluate, particularly if the failure of one segment leads to the failure of others. In risk assessment, this is known as **common-mode failure**: a tendency for separable portions of a system or project to be represented as having independent failure probabilities when in fact an underlying common-cause failure potential is present.

- **Categorical exclusion (CE) bundling***:* Under some circumstances rangers may use the CE approach to bundle a number of small projects into an overall project that may be marginally appropriate for the CE designation. This approach may actually increase process risk (particularly with respect to the agency internal NEPA review process in that the characteristics of the project could warrant an EA) in favor of potentially reducing risks to the natural resource base. Some rangers may view the internal NEPA review process as a separate source of process risk. This management strategy has a proactive stance toward accomplishing work on the land. It is highly dependent upon an individual ranger's risk-taking propensity, tolerance for risk, and perception of the downside associated with an unfavorable review of their use of the CE mechanism.

- **Early and extensive involvement of nonfederal stakeholders***:* Rangers may engage a variety of publics as part of both defining project scope and building stakeholder agreement as a strategy for reducing process risk. Publics engaged may include the general public as well as particular constituencies that could or do have objections or concerns about a (potential) proposed management action. Nonfederal stakeholders also may be engaged as part of a general discussion or elicitation of views about resource management and, for example, community needs that can be satisfied by unit-initiated projects.

*"I tend not to select projects that will take years and years to do. By the time you take a 5-year project and put the decision out, you got some issue that's hit and your analysis has failed. I look at projects that are efficient and can be done in smaller chunks."*

### Barriers to NEPA process efficiency—

The staging and management of staff work may be an important contributor to NEPA process inefficiencies. Staff specialists are called upon for a variety of tasks,

*"The reason NEPA takes a lot of time is because we have our specialists busy on so many things and so spread out that it's hard for them to focus on a project, get it to a certain point, and then move on and do something next. They're constantly interrupted by other priorities."*

*"Part of the job that I have to do is balance what we have available as far as total resource and budget, and how much of a risk a particular resource is in the big picture."*

*"I want a really good reason to be doing this. I don't want a sloppy, uncertain reason to do this. I want confidence that it's worth it."*

of which NEPA-related analyses are only one. Interruptions in the analysis process may produce significant gaps in staff workflow, possibly leading to inefficiencies when staff must start-stop-restart, for example, an EA.

Obsolescence before completion occurs when an analysis takes such a long period of calendar time that critical assumptions or information in an analysis are no longer valid and the analysis has to be started anew. Staff turnover on long-running analysis can require redoing all or significant parts of an analysis.

The distribution of NEPA expertise is not uniform across management units. Although some ranger districts may have a key NEPA staff member, others may have to rely on either a shared resource at the forest (or higher) level, while still others may have NEPA expertise that is on the margin of being outdated.

Risk attitudes differ across rangers and management situations. The incentive structure and value for taking risks as part of management decisionmaking is not always clear. A 2005 study of line officers' perceptions of agency values found that risk taking and innovation were among the least rewarded values (Kennedy et al. 2005). National Environmental Policy Act projects represent opportunities for innovation as well as potential exposure to risks. How innovation is rewarded, and line officers are indemnified or protected against losses to their unit associated with the NEPA process, will be a factor in determining both the projects that they choose to develop and the methods they use to help ensure that they and their unit do not experience loss associated with process risk.

**Line officer decisionmaking and the NEPA process—**
Line officers may differ in how they define and describe their decisionmaking process. For some line officers, the decision regarding which project alternative to propose may be made very early in the project development process. In some cases, the line officer may have a particular (and focused) management action in mind from the very beginning of project development and through the NEPA process. This tendency may interact with the characteristics of a particular project or type of project, and a given line officer may not be consistent in the degree to which their initial formulation of a project focuses on a clearly identified and preferred management action.

For other line officers, the decision regarding which project alternative to propose may emerge from the NEPA process and their interaction with project staff during the development of NEPA documentation. They may begin a project with a generalized sense or idea of a desirable management action, and use pre-NEPA as well as NEPA process interactions with staff to refine and hone their preferred alternative.

Still other line officers may view the best decision in terms of what actually gets implemented and may take a larger perspective on the NEPA process that includes appeals and litigation as additional elements that shape and define the best alternative to pursue. In these situations, line officers may be less concerned about overall process risk and may work to move projects through to a decision more quickly. These line officers may view the overall NEPA process, including its judicial appeal and review elements, as a negotiation process in which multiple cycles of planning, proposal development, public scoping and judicial review are needed to produce a final, implemented project. For these line officers, a successful project may be defined in terms of a socially acceptable outcome that meets the needs and values of a variety of stakeholder perspectives.

*"The process that you went through to produce it is where you get the confidence in the EA."*

Decision confidence is of significant importance to line officers, as they must speak for the project to audiences and constituents both inside and outside of the agency. Line officer management of the NEPA process and the work of their staff is a significant source of confidence in decisionmaking and goes beyond the information content of the NEPA documentation (e.g., EA). Line officers may have only general familiarity with the detailed information and analytical content of, for example, an environmental analysis, and rely upon their staff specialists as well as their confidence in those specialists as disciplinary experts to support their conclusions about the soundness and rigor of the analysis. Familiarity with and control of the management process by which an environmental analysis is created provides assurance that the chosen management action is the best action from all possible actions that could be proposed.

*"The main thing (for me) is knowing . . . the decision I'm about to make is supported by all the specialist input and what I know."*

## Summary and Recommendations

This exploratory study used interviews with district rangers to identify concepts that may be of use in understanding how resource management projects are initiated and developed, and how management activities associated with project development may be influenced by aspects of the NEPA process. The application of more rigorous and structured methodological approaches is needed to determine the validity and utility of the concepts identified here. These approaches could include interview-based methods that explore indepth the management experiences of individual rangers. If there is a single message that can be delivered from this initial work it is this: enormous variability may exist in the district ranger population, some owing to context, some to individuals' backgrounds and management styles, and some to how the complexities of managing a ranger district are interpreted and applied to resource management decisionmaking. At a minimum, a census is needed to determine the extent of this variability and its impact on how projects are developed. Survey-based approaches using either traditional, mail-out survey methods or Web-based protocols can be used to conduct such a census.

The present study has identified a number of concepts that offer potential value for further research. The concept of **process risk** may be an important assessment that guides many of the decisions associated with selecting, conceptualizing, developing, and analyzing NEPA projects. This rich and informal assessment has no standardized guidelines and is subjected to some of the same sources of variability that may be inherent in other dimensions of the ranger population. How individual rangers conduct this assessment and apply its results will influence the projects they choose to pursue, and determine those that they reject. How they gauge the risks to themselves and their unit associated with the NEPA process and how they manage those risks will be an important driver in the efficiency they are able to attain in moving projects from an initial starting point through the NEPA process to useful action on the ground.

The concept of the NEPA triangle (fig. 1) as a metaphor for carrying out the NEPA process in the context of unit management may not reflect (a) the complexities of addressing the multiobjective nature of unit management, which includes management of human resources, financial resources, and natural resources and (b) the way in which district rangers actually do their work in concert with their staff and their upper level management. The linear representation of the NEPA process portrayed by the NEPA triangle does not account for the nonlinear and iterative approach that district rangers (often) use to accomplish the development of a project, its required documentation, and the consensus-style management that is often used to bring both line and staff into agreement about the best management alternative to pursue for a given project. In addition, the NEPA triangle has significant but unacknowledged hooks or linkages to other important elements of the larger NEPA process that includes appeals and litigation, the outcomes of which have important consequences for unit functioning.

Prior to the existence of NEPA, district rangers had considerable latitude to make resource management decisions and execute resource management plans with relatively little encumbrance by documentation and process requirements or by the need to work collaboratively with nonagency stakeholders. One of the adaptive management responses to NEPA has been for the ranger cadre to move from a command-and-control style of management to a consensus style of management that requires rangers who are more skilled and comfortable with a highly interactive management style that focuses on process, inclusion, and collaboration.

Research has pointed out that although rangers still oversee projects on the ground, they also serve as facilitators of public dialogue about forest management policy within their communities (Apple 1996, Tipple and Wellman 1991).

A consequence of the distributional change in the amount of unit work that is needed to support process-related activities, such as meetings, written communications, documentation, stakeholder outreach, and the like results in an adaptive shift in how line management candidates are selected and developed. Today's ranger population may be more oriented to the planning and analysis aspects of project development than yesterday's rangers, who were more inclined toward action and outcome cycles and for whom the ideal decision tempo was more fast paced. Ideally, these two concepts can be merged into an efficient amalgam of process sensitivity, collaborative project development, and adaptive management that emphasizes the need for focused action and response cycles.

Although the NEPA document itself was not a focal point of this study, it is a significant factor in the overall cost, efficiency, and outcome of the NEPA process. Since the inception of NEPA, the documentation process has expanded considerably, with today's NEPA documents containing highly detailed analysis of project alternatives and their impacts. But what of the need for the project in the first place and full consideration of the "no action" alternative? Has NEPA documentation kept pace with the need to inform a broad constituency, including the general public as well as specialized readers such as congressional staffers, about the value and benefit of a project or a program of work? More broadly, on whose behalf is the NEPA analysis and documentation done? Who is the audience? There is reason to believe that in the maelstrom of NEPA documentation requirements, these fundamental questions of audience have gotten misplaced, if not lost. The need for a project is a significant aspect of how many organizations develop their environmental reporting documentation.[3] Some organizations have adopted a model of developing highly readable executive summaries in which the need for the project forms a core for communicating an environmental analysis.[4] We propose greater

---

[3] Private industry must comply with environmental reporting requirements for many of their projects. For example, some states have environmental disclosure requirements modeled on NEPA. Need for a project is a key element of many private industry environmental analyses. The "no action" alternative may be richly developed in terms such as projections from current conditions to points in the future both without and with the project under consideration.

[4] The National Aeronautics and Space Administration has for some of its NEPA documents developed focused and highly-readable executive summaries that synthesize the content of, for example, an EIS and at the same time articulate the need for action. The intended readership for these documents includes the general public as well as, for example, congressional staffers.

emphasis on "need for the project" in analysis, and a much richer description of the projected impacts of the "no action" alternative. The NEPA document needs to be more synchronized with the needs, interests, and capabilities of specific audiences and readerships, including general and specialized publics, congressional staffers, the judiciary, and the media at large. Focused effort needs to be placed on reviewing and identifying how NEPA documentation could be improved as a vehicle for communicating and furthering the agency's multiuse mission.

Many of the challenges the agency faces today in terms of the NEPA process arise, in part, from the contentiousness that is experienced in the public arena with respect to the desirability of proposed agency actions. A significant part of this discord arises from differences of opinion concerning the value of active management of natural resources. Not everyone agrees that active management of natural resources is desirable. For some, human intrusion into natural processes is objectionable and they prefer passive management, by which nature is allowed to take its own course. But, belief in the desirability of active management is a predicate for a positive response to a NEPA project proposal. At the extreme of disbelief, all NEPA projects are rejected on principle. For those in the middle, which is the broad public and nongovernmental organization stakeholder constituency, "active" may have varying definitions and may be fluid depending on the circumstances. In these cases, which are the majority, the agency has an opportunity to define its position and the value of active management of natural resources. It must take this opportunity each time it is available and not assume that the value is firm and consistent in the minds of stakeholders. One of the more available places this challenge can be met is in NEPA documentation and through the NEPA process.

## Acknowledgments

Support for this project was provided by the USDA Forest Service, Pacific Northwest Research Station, Focused Science Delivery Program under Agreement No. 06-JV-11261976-297 to MacGregor-Bates, Inc. A preliminary version of this paper was presented at the *NEPA for the 21st Century, Workshop on Integration of NEPA Processes*, Stevenson, WA, March 19-22, 2007. We would like to acknowledge the various reviewers for the publication as their comments provided clarity on several issues and enhanced the final product. Reviews were completed by individuals with a scientific and research background as well as individuals with a land management and line officer background. We would like to extend our sincere gratitude to the individual line officers who provided us the benefit of their knowledge and extensive experience in support of this study. They are listed below with their unit association at the time of their interview: Ken Anderson, Wallowa-Whitman National Forest, Whitman Unit, Baker City, OR; Bill Anthony, Deschutes National Forest, Sisters Ranger District, Sisters, OR; Dave Campbell, Bitterroot National Forest, South Fork Ranger District, Darby, MT; Erin Connelly, Rogue River National Forest, Applegate Ranger District, Jacksonville, OR; Roberto Delgado, Six Rivers National Forest, Mad River Ranger District, Mad River, CA; Cliff Dils, Umpqua National Forest, Roseburg, OR; Doug Gochnour, Boise National Forest, Idaho City Ranger District, Idaho City, ID; Chuck Hagerdon, Cibola National Forest, Mt. Taylor Ranger District, Grants, NM; Lisa Krueger, Flathead National Forest, Tally Lake Ranger District, Whitefish, MT; Cindy Lane, Clearwater National Forest, Kooskia Ranger District, Kooskia, ID; Maggie Pittman, Lolo National Forest, Missoula Ranger District, Missoula, MT; Alan Vandiver, Klamath National Forest, Happy Camp and Oak Knoll Ranger District, Happy Camp, CA.

# Literature Cited

**Apple, D.D. 1996.** Changing social and legal forces affecting the management of national forests. Women in Natural Resources. 18: 1–13.

**Arkes, H.; Blumer, C. 1985.** The psychology of sunk cost. Organizational Behavior and Human Decision Processes. 35: 124–140.

**Arkes, H.; Hutzel, L. 2000.** The role of probability of success estimates in the sunk cost effect. Journal of Behavioural Decision Making. 13: 295–306.

**Bernstein, P.L. 1998**. Against the gods: the remarkable story of risk. New York: John Wiley & Sons.

**Cashmore, M. 2004.** The role of science in environmental impact assessment: process and procedure versus purpose in the development of theory. Environmental Impact Assessment Review. 24: 403–426.

**Cleaves, D.A.; Haynes, R.W. 1999**. Risk management for ecological stewardship. In: Sexton, W.T.; Malk, A.J.; Szaro, R.C.; Johnson, N.C., eds. Ecological stewardship: a common reference for ecosystem management. Oxford, United Kingdom: Elsevier Science, Ltd.: 431–461. Vol. 3.

**Fischhoff, B.; Lichtenstein, S.; Slovic, P.; Derby, S.; Keeney, R. 1981.** Acceptable risk. Cambridge, MA: Cambridge University Press. 193 p.

**Haimes, Y. 1998.** Risk modeling, assessment, and management. New York: Wiley & Sons. 744 p.

**Jesse, L. 1998.** The National Environmental Policy Act Net (NEPANET) and DOE NEPA Web: what they bring to environmental impact assessment. Environmental Impact Assessment Review. 18: 73–82.

**Kahneman, D.; Tversky, A. 1979.** Prospect theory: an analysis of decision under risk. Econometrica. 47: 263–291.

**Kaplan, S.; Garrick, B. 1981.** On the quantitative definition of risk. Risk Analysis. 17: 407–417.

**Kaufman, H. 1960.** The forest ranger: a study in administrative behavior. Baltimore, MD: Johns Hopkins University Press. 259 p.

**Kennedy, J.J.; Haynes, R.W.; Zhou, X. 2005.** Line officers' views on stated USDA Forest Service values and the agency reward system. Gen. Tech. Rep. PNW-GTR-632. Portland, OR: U.S. Department of Agriculture, Forest Service, Pacific Northwest Research Station. 72 p.

**Kennedy, J.J.; Krannich, R.S.; Quigley, T.M.; Cramer, L.S. 1992.** How employees view the USDA-Forest Service value and reward system. Logan, UT: Department of Forest Resources, Utah State University. 62 p.

**Koontz, T.M. 2007.** Federal and state public forest administration in the new millennium: revisiting Herbert Kaufman's The Forest Ranger. Public Administration Review. 67: 152–164.

**Laband, D.N.; Gonzalez-Caban, A.; Hussain, A. 2006.** Factors that influence administrative appeals of proposed USDA Forest Service fuels reduction actions. Forest Science. 52: 476–488.

**Luther, L. 2005.** The National Environmental Policy Act: background and implementation. CRS Report for Congress. Congressional Research Service–The Library of Congress. Order Code RL33152. November 16, 2005. 38 p.

**Magill, A.W. 1991.** Barriers to effective public interaction: helping natural resource professionals adjust their attitudes. Journal of Forestry. 89: 16–18.

**Markowitz, H. 1959.** Portfolio selection: efficient diversification of investments. New Haven, CT: Yale University Press. 344 p.

**Martin, W.E.; Shields, D.J.; Tolwinski, B.; Kent, B. 1996.** An application of social choice theory to USDA Forest Service decision making. Journal of Policy Modeling. 18: 603–621.

**Montgomery, H.; Lipschitz, R.; Brehmer, B. 2004.** How professionals make decisions. Mahwah, NJ: Lawrence Erlbaum Associates. 472 p.

**National Environmental Policy Act [NEPA]. 2003.** 40 C.F.R. § 1500.1(c).

**Thompson, T.L. 2007.** A historical analysis of consolidation at the national forest and district level in the U.S. Forest Service. T. L. Thompson Consulting, L.L.C. [Pagination unknown].

**Tipple, T.J.; Wellman, J.D. 1991.** Herbert Kaufman's forest ranger thirty years later: from simplicity and homogeneity to complexity and diversity. Public Administration Review. 51: 421–428.

**U.S. Department of Agriculture, Forest Service [USDA Forest Service]. 2002.** The process predicament: how statutory, regulatory, and administrative factors affect national forest management. Washington, DC. 40 p.

**U.S. Department of Agriculture, Forest Service [USDA Forest Service]. 2007.** Forest Plan Implementation Course 1900–01. http://fsweb.wo.fs.fed.us/am/ nepa/nepa_coordination_training/00index.html. (October 2007).

**Wilde, G. 2001.** Target Risk 2. Toronto, ON: PDE Publications. 255 p.

**Yaffee, S.L. 1999.** Three faces of ecosystem management. Conservation Biology. 13: 713–725.

www.ingramcontent.com/pod-product-compliance
Lightning Source LLC
Chambersburg PA
CBHW080751290526
45790CB00008B/3407